With Healing in His Wings

Written by Amber Everett
Cover art and layout by Alexie Olivares

To the saviors, who do more good than they know.

Introduction

My friend,

If I could ask God for one thing today, knowing undoubtedly that He'd grant it to me, I'd ask Him for the chance to sit beside you; to cry, feel, and bask together in the face of what we've lost. I've found that our pain is quieted when we do not bear it alone.

If we did sit side-by-side today, there are a few things I would want you to know.

The first is that you are loved; more deeply than ever you may know. Your life holds intrinsic value and worth; your very soul exudes a light that is pure, untouched, and worthy of love. *You* are worthy of love.

The second is that wherever you are, in whatever darkness you may find yourself, you are not alone. It is likely that there are friends and saviors around you now, working hard to lift and love you through your pain. If that is not true, fear not; for the Lord our God is always with us. He will never forsake us in our darkness. Though love, light, peace, and healing may feel far from you now, I can promise they are not. These things are coming to you fast, friend; sometimes you just have to weather the last shades of storm before they can filter through the clouds and reach you.

In thinking of loss, of hope, of light and life, I am reminded of an Angels & Airwaves song that begins:

When all is said and done
Will we still feel pain inside?
Will all these scars go away with night?
Stars smile for the morning light
It's like the best dream to have
Where everything is not so bad
And every tear is so alone
Like God himself is coming home
To say I
I can do anything, if you want me here
And I can fix anything, if you'll let me near
Where are those secrets now
That you're just scared to tell
I'll whisper them all aloud
So you can hear yourself

With Healing in His Wings tells the story of my brother, Joshua, who took his life and fell from darkness into light. He lives there now, in light, while we live on without him.

More than a tale of loss though, these words tell of my friends, my saviors, who carried me through my personal darkness into gracious light. I dedicate this story to them, and to my God, my one true Savior: Brother, Healer, Light, and Friend.

May His light be a sure beacon to you, too, in dark places.

In hope,
Amber

Part I
Pupa

1
Josh

The world spins on its axis, drooping in space with the weight of all our grief.

Today, it crashes down with the weight of mine.

I am alone, sitting atop the gray steps of a grassy park. Tears well at my eyes and though there are people around—walking, laughing, and playing with dogs—I cannot hold my sobs in. They break from me in waves, rack my frame and flip me dizzy in the head. *Josh*, I think.

Josh.

Annie asks why I came to work today; then, after a few moments of confusion, I clamor, "I didn't expect it to affect me this much." My words drip raw with guilt.

"But I live nearby. Can you drop me off?"

We drive past streets and familiar houses, though this time things are different. My throbbing head pulls them towards me, around me, causes windows and blades and signs to encase me like lead. My very organs constrict inwards—intestines wrap my lungs and heart, sucking the simple, quiet life out of me.

"I'm right here," I say.

I enter my bedroom as thoughts begin to leak from every pore. I think of black, of red, anything beyond this gray. I wish for prayer, peace, relief, but nothing will come. A single thought torpedoes back and forth across my skull:

Josh, I think.

Josh.

What is it you've done, my brother?

2
Train

It is a placid evening in August when the call comes.

Night hits and I'm weary, waiting under the humming light of a train station, as my phone buzzes stark white.

"Are you sitting down?" my mom asks through the receiver. "Make sure you're sitting down for this."

Queasy. Cold hands. Breathless heart.

"What?" I ask. "What's wrong?"

My train arrives and, with the other passengers, I step in as questions burst red from my scalp.

"Amber?" my mom asks.

"Amber?"

"Yes?"

"Did you hear me? I said Joshua shot himself."

What?

My eyes close and I rub the crown of my nose. All the world is whirling.

"What do you mean?"

"Your brother shot himself tonight. He's dead."

I hang up and look out the window. There, in the darkness, reigns one choking black void where sky should be.

Only one torrid white bullet speeds through the darkness:

My train—

His choice—

And my form simply breaks. Josh is gone.

3
Joy

Joy comes first. I exit the train and stagger to her house, sick, black and blue from the day's battering. I find her there waiting.

"What's going on?" she asks. Her voice speaks concern while a slight Nebraska twang brings gilded comfort to my ears. I love my friend Joy.

I step forward to speak but, burdened with exhaustion and a frenzied, emerging shakiness, my words fade. Both eyes blink raw and I can't breathe.

"Joy," I simply say. She doesn't know, hasn't heard yet, but she hears me. Joy understands.

Inside her house lives a dull blue couch where we sit. Joy smiles, listens, but her expression grows serious as we talk.

"May I ask which family member?" she questions.

"My brother," I say.

"Amber," she replies softly. Then, silence.

"I'm so sorry."

"I'm so

so

so sorry."

And Joy is. We all are.

4
Casket

With help, my two remaining brothers, aged eleven and sixteen, carry Josh's casket to his grave.

I see it and think, *this box is too small, too impossible to hold Josh and all that he was in life.*

While it could not have held all he was in life, it seems in death it is sufficient.

5
Details

The details are many. I quickly find that like flies, they buzz and thump at the walls of my mind, prod me with beams and wings and antennae. *Let us freeee,* they say, *we want to be freeeeeee.*

No, I tell them. Persistent, I swat at them, watch as they leave gooey black bug smears across the soft pinks of my brain. *You are mine,* I tell them. *Mine to do with as I please.*

And what I say is true: they aren't going anywhere.

6
Choice

Brother,

I have tried hard to be couth, but I must be honest with you now:

Your choice disgusts me. Not the choice itself, not its reality, but what you've done with it. *Certainly* what you've done with it. I think of you and my chest quivers—

Do you know what you've done to us?

If you did, would you still have done it?

Yes, Josh, yes. I believe you still would have.

7
Blame

In considering it, I suppose we are to blame. Your family members and friends—the ones who loved you; hated you; broke for you and with you and in spite of you; the ones who lie heavy and lifeless now in the choice you've made for us all. We hold your loaded gun and carry it—cold, metallic, lifeless—to your firing grounds. *Pew pew — pew pew pew pew pew.* Are you happy? Are you happy now, Josh?

You've stamped your legacy into plaster. It's painted red and white on the walls of your bedroom: bone and gristle and bare life—mind and body blown black—faceless struggle raging against the carpet, ceiling, your old splattered bedposts and things. They cleared your room of belongings, but we kept your PlayStation, this wretched machine that swallowed so much of your waking self. You taught us all the good ones—shooting games 1, 2, 3, ghosts, and zombies. Your impact is measured, now, in the number of undead we round up and slaughter.

Sometimes we still play games in your absence, though none of us can manage to top your high score.

8
Love

I do not bear my grief alone.

The night after Josh dies, I reach out to a good family friend and his sweetheart wife with a bold, simple plea:

Please help. My brother shot himself last night.

They call back right away.

"Where are you right now?" they ask. Then, without waiting for my answer, "We are coming to get you."

I pack my bag and wait on the curb for them to show up, my two loving surrogate parents while mine are far away. Fortitude fades as I see their car arrive.

"Let us carry that for you," they say.

We drive to their home, a place as warm as any I have known. A prayer is offered, a pronouncement of peace, and I am left alone to grieve. I climb upstairs, curl up in a corner, and sob for hours.

Late into the evening, a note slips under my door. *We will be down in the family room for a little while if you want to talk,* it reads.

Face red and puffy from tears, I determine to brave the downstairs. I clear my face as best I can, breathe in a huff of life-sustaining air, and head down to join them.

"Do you want ice cream?" they ask me immediately upon my entry. "We have three different kinds."

Cold bowls in hand, we sit in the family room and talk—shoot the breeze about boys, Colorado, and the funny things in life. It's a moment bright and filled with simple peace. *I am happy here,* I realize. *And here, with these friends, I am loved.*

Here, I am held. I am safe.

9
Pop-Tart Casserole

The sweetness doesn't end there. Two sisters of mine—friends and candid saviors—bake a Pop-Tart casserole and bring it to me the very next week. Without my having to speak, to ask, to cry, they discern what I need most and offer their love to me without words.

Thankfully for me, their love comes in strawberry.

"A casserole," I say one day when Joy asks how others can help. "My family has been given the strangest casseroles since Josh passed away, and really, all I need is a casserole to help get me through this."

Joy nods, contemplative. "Are you still living off of Pop-Tarts?" she asks.

"You know it," I reply. Then, thinking of the fine, sugary goodnesses, I smirk. "Pop-Tarts are life."

Delivered later that night, I come home to a warm, happy, heartfelt confection. My eyes fill with wonder. *How did they do it?* I think, as fresh strawberries quickly cover my lips. *How?* Delighted,

I slice myself another square, two, three, and head off to my room. There, alone and three bites in, I place my fork delicately on the plate, lay them both carefully on the ground, cover my face with my hands, and weep.

Lips sworn sweet in strawberry, cheeks in tears, I pause to feel: loved; known; whole, for a good long moment. *My sweet friends,* I simply think. *My sweet, sweet friends.*

What friends and saviors they are to me.

10
Mix

In the mix of peace, sorrow, and grief that follows Josh's death, I determine to move home to Nevada. I meet with Joy on a dusty baseball field to share the news.

"I need to take time to heal and find peace," I tell her. She nods understandingly. "I love you, Amb," she says. "I hope you find what you need there."

My feet kick up sand beneath us, send fogs of dust into clear, clear air. I won't look at her.

"So do I," I respond quietly.

Part II
Cocoon

11
Cascade

Wasps cascade against the windows of my car, ooze strings of gooey black slime across the glass. It's dark but whiffs of yellow-black—bees—clump around the handles, muffler, mirrors. *Go away!* I shout—*Go away!* Amid the frenzied hum of insect wings, my words emerge just a frail whimper. *Please*, I try instead. *Please, please, go away.*

I'm parked alone in red, in black, at a kind of cathedral not far from home. I sensed the darkness, heard it swarming, felt to flee here first. In swatches, these came too. Through panels of wings and limbs I catch the gold, the gilded lightness of a burning white building behind the madness. *Aghhfgah*, I hear as they rush against my window, again and again. *Afghfabghahh.*

It's been one month in this city now, city of lights, one month seeking "life" and "light" and "opportunity" but finding only illness. Not one but two spiders clamber over my things, scale my walls like cretins as I ponder this. They stop to watch me from their spindly webs and, yes, here, we understand one another.

Days turned to weeks while the humming started. They came first as gnats but quickly grew—to flies to bees to wasps. Hordes would pound at my door, at my door, at my door—begging to be let in. *Hello?* they'd say to me, *Hello?* They never seemed to understand, really, who was welcome here.

Then, best I could when things grew hard, I'd run; and, on days like these, find myself parked, entangled in red and black near white but never never close enough. Too far to save me from the swarms of scalding wings, come to me in light, in darkness, in day, rest, or nightmare.

The wings always found me. What did not, it seems, was my God. Where was He? Could He still find me through this storm of madness?

Though I wanted so badly to believe it, my heart's courage faded in blackness.

12
Hitting

It's two days later, alone in my apartment, when the hitting starts.

This one's thoughts; more memories than thoughts; more fear, trauma, and pain than memories. They beat down on me like:

You did it

You did it

You killed him

YOU KILLLLLLLED HIM

Your one and only brother, Josh

How could you, Amber

Oh my gosh, Amber

How could you

He's dead, dead

DEAD DEAD DEAD DEAD DEAD DEAD

deEaeAaAaDdeAAaaeaeEEddd

Hahhah!

Knock knock knock knock knock, I'm here

Here outside that bathroom that you're shaking in

Here outside the door you're locked in and won't touch again for

Hoooooouuuuuuuurrrrrsssssss

Hello, hello

I know you can hear me

I know you are here

Here

Heere

Alone and, and—

Alone, and

Bump bump bump bump bump bump bump

"STOP!" I shout—*"GO AWAY!"*

It's my mind turned against me but tonight, it's unrelenting. I waste my life curled loud in a corner, a burning head my only noise, only light in this godforsaken apartment I'm not going to leave… for fear that my life might just keep going on this way.

Amber, my thoughts say. *Aaaaaaamber.*

My heart stays quiet and just takes it.

13
Doctor

"So tell me, Amber, how've you been?"

"I've been alright."

"Just alright?"

Images: *a flash*

cerebral thunder, drums

raindrops, raindrops, falling on limbs in day, in broad day, trickling down and casting scars like burn marks where they touch

a nightmare,

nightmare

a nother and nother and noth—

"Amber?"

"Sorry. Yes. I've been busy. Trying to keep on top of projects and such."

"I'm glad to hear you've been keeping yourself busy. How

are classes?"

HAH. Classes.

"Good," I say.

"Any new updates?"

Yes. Every day feels like a hurricane and my hair whips my face like nothing you've ever seen, scrawls through my eyes and chunks of brain like it's nothing and leaves me falling, fearless, paralyzed in stripe and strip and this nasty nasty blaze of stark-white indecision. If only I could tell, could tell, could tell tell tell tell tell you—

"No."

"Okay. Thank you for sharing. Now, why don't we try something new today?"

She goes on. It's a session like all others, where I go and learn "skills" to "confront my grief," "take hold of my future," and "lean into the pain" that I'm feeling. As always, I stay as long as I can bear then leave, step outside into the stark, stark whiteness of day, where the contrast of guilt and shame weigh heavy in my mind, on my shoulders, begins to soak through my paper-thin clothes like sweat. It's cool outside but my head burns—a dull, screaming pain that never stops, manifests itself only in a sufferance of courage, grace, love and connection. *All is well*, I rehearse simply. *All is well.*

As always, I drive home slowly; and, alone with the quiet of just my own voice, work hard to drown out the rainfall of tears that commences.

14
Lost

A few weeks in I realize: not all is lost.

I meet a bishop, here, in this city of lights—a minister, servant, protector of some kind, though I just call him "father." Another caring, stand-in dad while mine is home and far away.

Though he has three of his own, he stops to take me in, along with others he knows are struggling. I reason his sons and daughters must walk all across the globe now.

He speaks to me as a father, tells me he's lost someone too. The very same week, even, that Josh disappeared.

"Sister Everett," he begins. It's a name he uses sweetly because I'm daughter, friend, family here. "Where is your mind at today?" he asks. He phrases it as a question though his tone suggests he knows the answer already.

"Well I've certainly felt better," I say with half a smile.

He returns it and nods. Father tells me of his daughter, lost in tragic summer, and about the light she poured fully into this world. I can tell I've missed much in never having met her.

Our discussion turns to Josh, to grief.

"I've read just about every book on death I can find," Father says, "though nothing has brought peace to me." The words are stated as truth, not complaint. I sense a glimpse and see: in his eyes lives a depth of sadness not even my weary heart can fathom.

"I wonder if your efforts have yielded different."

My heart breaks for this man, this dad, who I know is hurting so much. I think of where my search for peace has led but stop; breathe. It's a sordid well of darkness I don't want to draw from today.

"I don't know if peace always comes in this lifetime," I say. They're words I've been taught from childhood, though a truth or a lie, perhaps, that my soul yearns not to believe. Father looks at me and thinks for a moment.

"Well, Sister Everett," he begins, "as you are here alone in this city, grieving the loss of your brother, I suggest we move through this grief process together..."

His words continue, as do mine, though the specifics of our conversation fade, leave a feeling of the burgeoning, quiet beginnings of hope.

For the first time in months, I feel it: a sense of not being all alone in this darkness; a sense that all the sorrow in the world is not just mine to bear; and, then—

The sweet awareness of having a friend, father, and savior to weather my grief with me.

15
Family

Here in the city of lights, I become part of a family.

How it happens is painful, though there's spirit and journey in the pain. "Sister Bluely passed away this week," Father tells us one Sunday morning. "She died in a car accident."

I don't know this girl, didn't meet her before she passed, though the respectful quiet and visceral pain of the listening audience tells me that she was a sister and daughter to be loved.

"We'd like anyone available to sing at her funeral."

Before my brain remembers that I cannot carry a single tune on key, my heart fills with courage and my hand rises. "I'll sing," I say.

For another sibling of mine lost in sorrow, I think, *I'll sing.* In this moment I don't say it, but know it, rather:

Sometimes our toneless voices are all we have to bind us through the sorrow.

16
Girl in Blue

Days later the chapel burns brightly, lightly, quiet with the morning. Its children filter in.

Sister Bluely's father is first, come to thank us for our voices. Her mother, then, tearless and silent. Aunts, uncles, cousins, and friends filter in, here to show support for this fiery, bursting star of a girl. Others, like me, sit quietly and observe. Though we did not know her, there's a blurring, unfathomable love that fills every atom of air.

I never met you, Girl in Blue, I think, *but today I can see that you are loved beyond belief. These ones are here not to mourn, but to celebrate you and all that you were in life.*

Your journey was one to be reckoned with.

Quietly, I sit humming a hymn to myself, page 192 in the book I'm holding.

Verse two sounds and I stop, realize with suddenness that I am not alone—no. Instead, I am held in wisdom and confidence by Father, who knows me and has come to comfort me in this day of our grief.

"Thinking about brother?" Father asks as I close the book, turn towards his face. He's placed a strong arm around my shoulder to remind me that he's there, that I'm safe and loved here in this place. I nod, happy to have him near.

Josh lives heavy in my mind, his skin and memory choked with a sadness that's thicker than usual. "I miss him," I say. It's a moment of undoubted blue truth, but the words are sharp in my voice and heart. It's true: I do miss my brother.

Father nods. We sit in silence for a time.

Then he begins, "When I think of our loved ones who have passed on, I believe they see us. See the things we're doing." My thoughts pause as I listen intently.

"I think if your brother could see you now, singing at the funeral of a girl you've never met, he'd be proud." The last word is spoken but already, my sight is swallowed in tears. Sorrow boils inside me—blue, blue, blue—drains down my face and hands in a wretched display of grief, true but held close for far too long. There is much I want to say but the words burn bigger than I am; instead, I breathe and allow myself to cry for a moment. Father holds me in his kind, strong arms to let me know he is there.

I miss him so much, I think of Josh, the words a healing balm, today, against the blue of my mind. I cannot speak them all, but I know Father knows and hears me all the same.

The moment endures as Sister Bluely's procession commences. I move up the chapel steps as the choir is called, dressed solid in blue today, to sing our anthem to this child, lost in life. I'm choked with tears before the song even begins, though still my voice rises triumphant with the others. "Be still, my soul," our quiet hymn begins...

Be still, my soul: The Lord is on thy side
With patience bear thy cross of grief or pain
Leave to thy God to order and provide;
In ev'ry change he faithful will remain.
Be still, my soul: Thy best, thy heav'nly Friend
Thru thorny ways leads to a joyful end

Be still, my soul: Thy God doth undertake
To guide the future as he has the past
Thy hope, thy confidence let nothing shake;
All now mysterious shall be bright at last.
Be still, my soul: The waves and winds still know
His voice who ruled them while he dwelt below

Be still, my soul: The hour is hast'ning on
When we shall be forever with the Lord,
When disappointment, grief, and fear are gone,
Sorrow forgot, love's purest joys restored.
Be still, my soul: When change and tears are past,

All safe and blessed we shall meet at last.

I step down from the stage with the others, enraptured in blue, and catch a glimpse of Father's eye as I do. Like brother, he, too, is proud.

He is proud, and so am I.

Part III
Imago

17
Flurry

I decide to move again, drive to Oregon in a flurry of madness and obsession. It isn't until I arrive—arms red, raw; face masked in salt; engine running entirely empty—that I calm down a bit, pause to take things in.

Here's what I see:

-A gas station

-Restaurants

-Oregon gas station man, filling up my tank for me

-Gas man watching with wonder as the digits continue to run up and up

-"Gosh, how did you not run out back on the highway?" he asks. "There's nothing in here!"

-"Oh, I've been running on empty a while," I say. "Gas never lasts long in this car."

And it's true, it doesn't.

18
Brand New

My new home is a shabby apartment in the heart of a rainy Oregon college town. Neighbor #1 is a Portlander—white with a ukulele and long brown dreads—a poster child for Oregon diversity. "Let me know if it ever gets too loud," she tells me, high on weed. "Sometimes I just get lost in the music, you know?"

I find a roommate to rent my second bedroom. It's three weeks before I find a mattress, thin and delivered straight to my home. Happy, I drag it to a corner, unroll it, and collapse, taking in my brand new life. *This is a good place*, I tell myself, *a good, good place*.

And, for a while, it is. I live bright in the outlands of a pain I'm hoping won't catch up to me.

19
Pokémon

It's sunny pre-autumn when I start to explore rain city. Then, without meaning to, I make friends.

El's is the first light to reach me through the rain. Quickly, I learn she sees things as I do and loves in a way bigger and bolder than I've known before. It's refreshing, this quick depth of friendship we establish.

We spend our time together at the dog park, waltzing the beach, getting pitas, laughing and talking all the while. One sunny afternoon we find ourselves caught downtown, catching Pokémon after Pokémon in the enticing wiles of suburbia.

"They designed this game for 12-year-old kids," I tell El as we step onto a crosswalk, heading towards the river. "Honestly, for children."

El's eyes stay glued to her phone as we cross, her index finger swiping meticulously to catch a Diglett that's burrowed up right there out of the asphalt. "I think you're just jealous that you can't throw a pokéball," El says.

"I throw pokéballs just fine," I reply with indignation. "But that's beside the point. Pokémon Go just isn't real Pokémon."

"A Lapras!!" El exclaims, ignoring my statement as we near the water. Her index finger moves fast towards her phone and she carefully selects a high-level pokéball to use. I shake my head.

"Let me catch this one," I say, hand reaching for the phone.

"No no, it's not worth the risk," El says, turning away from me. "I'll let you have the next one." El catches it first try.

Finally, El lets me hold her phone. We walk on and on, until, one lost Growlithe, three failed Caterpies, and 14 wasted pokéballs later, we arrive back at our cars. "I really enjoyed hanging out with you today," El begins.

"Same!" I respond. "We should do this again sometime."

It's a day of light and simplicity; and an hour that is, for us, one of many beginnings.

20
Talk

Weeks pass and I work hard to keep my struggles hidden from new friends. I go to activities, talk to people, work to make my presence known. Outside I'm short wavy hair, flannels, and the sick shark-attack longboard I carry everywhere I go. Beyond that, though, I can feel my mind twisting itself apart like fraying iron.

What do you mean? I ask in alarm, continuing an ongoing conversation between myself, my lighter and darker sides. I cower as dark-me takes the bait.

What are you doing? I'm asked.

Living, I reply. It seems obvious enough.

Why?

Because not all is lost yet. I have a chance at new life here. No one knows me or my story, things can be normal and I can build whatever kind of life I want.

You're living a lie, I hear; the words scald deep in my subconscious. *This darkness is your life.*

No, I respond, *it isn't. It can't be. Oregon is my chance for hope. For healing.*

Colorado, Nevada, and now Oregon? I'm reminded. *What were those? How many times have you grasped for re-invention and failed in putrid misery?*

That's not fair, I say. *It's different this time.*

What's different? dark-me asks. *Nothing. You're lying to yourself and you're lying to others. For years you've lived a lie you're still running from, you've murdered your brother through neglect and refuse now to face him in these dreams I send you every night.*

In these nightmares, I correct. *Josh shot himself. I had nothing to do with it.* I utter it, though even before the words ring through my heart wrenches; I don't believe it. Of course my neglect had everything to do with Josh's going away.

You're pathetic, I hear. The words start small but grow, rip through me into a dull, draining lull. *Pathetic. Pathetic pathetic pathetic.*

Can you please, just, stop? I ask.

Pathetic. Disgusting. I don't know what you're planning to do here. You have these wicked visions of the kind, generous person you want to be but we both know you're not that. You'll never *be that. You're less less less than the dust of the earth and will never be anything more. It's putrid—wretched—disgusting. Your brother is dead and you're to blame.*

No, I say, *I'm not*—and though I mean the words, they feel just wrong in my head.

Give up, I hear. *Give up. Give up give up give up! We both know that's all you're here to do anyway.*

No, I say, *no. Oregon is my chance for new life. For hope. Healing. Forgiveness.*

You're wild. You and I both know that the only life you'll ever have is—

—the words blur to madness here, blend into a debate that rips and tears my whole being in two. The devil and God rage inside me, rusted antlers rise to grind my heart like wasps, like sand, like a slow, fertile poison that drips and drains too much too fast.

I don't want to live this way, I speak simply. Despite the rage, the words live soft on my tongue. *I* won't *live this way,* I say.

Alone here in my heart of hearts, I follow my soft-spoken conviction with a prayer, kneel down and ask my God for a friend who will see me, hear me, help me. Someone to listen, hold, and guide me, again, towards hope.

Two years after Josh dies, God hears me… and He sends me one bursting answer to prayer.

21
Text

Hope comes as a response to a text, sent one bare November night:

Me:

Hey man, I won't be able to make it to church tomorrow

And just wanted to let you know

El:

Why???

Honestly I'm just really struggling right now. And it doesn't seem like a good idea.

I'm sorry. Struggling with what? If I may ask.

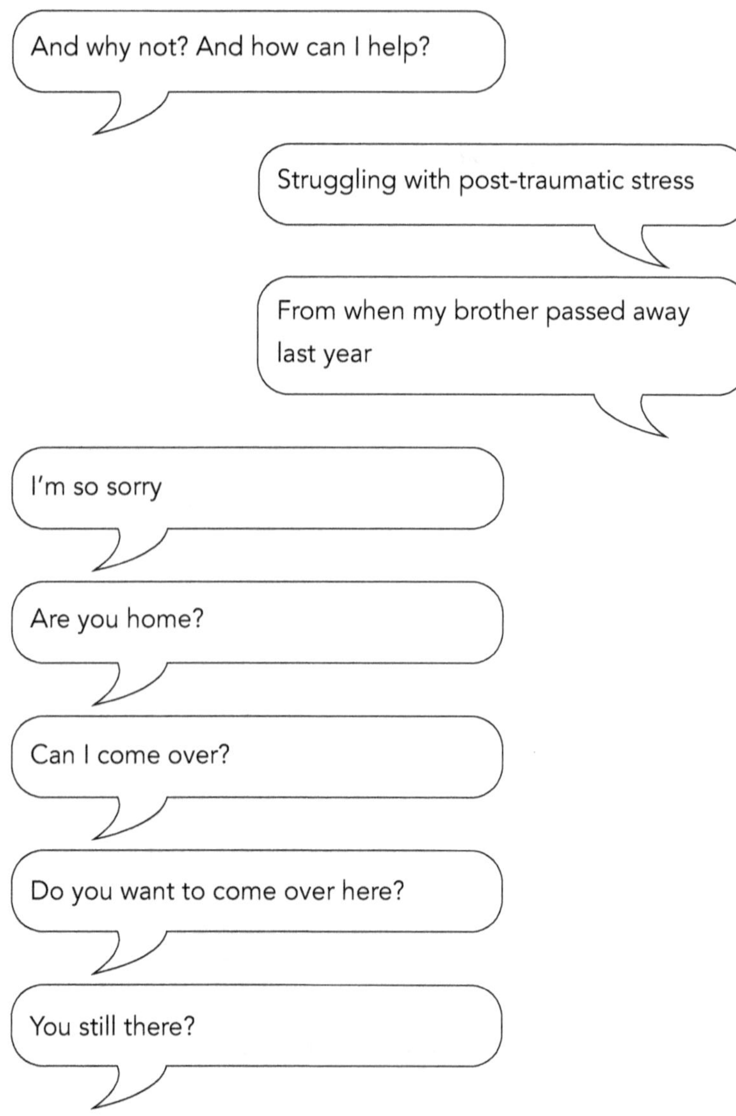

The line goes silent as I move outside. It's cold; I'm shaking; heart's held heavy in a lake of truth, trust, and vulnerability. I can't handle the notion that anyone might know my pain but me.

I spend an hour out in the cold, desperate. Then I return to find one more text:

Come on over. My cousin has vanilla ice cream

I go.

22
Warmth

I arrive at El's cousin's house shaky, afraid, and prickly with anxiety. This one's a first—another new beginning in our friendship.

El and I sit in the living room, near the fireplace. El's on the couch while I'm scrunched up on the floor—a position of my choosing—trying to breathe like a normal person. There's a sweet puggle named Lulu nearby who comes to check in on me from time to time. El waits patiently while I try try try, desperately, to find voice for my words. I'm unsuccessful, though El helps me through it.

"I don't know," I repeat continually as I watch slivers of wood twist, burn down in the fireplace. "It's something like post-traumatic stress but more. There are things that happen in your brain with something like this"—I can't use the word "suicide" here, though it's the one I mean—"that you just can't shut down. It's a fear, a constant fear, and I can't sleep and I'm not hungry and there's just this aching, aching grief all over that won't go away. Even on good days there's a blackness in my head that sucks me in like spider webs."

El looks at me and I see gray in the remains of a fire turned to ash. Sadness burns in her eyes and she simply says, "Amb, that sounds horrible. I am so, so, *so* sorry."

We talk more and watch a movie that night, and, while no greater words are said, I live warm and happy in the knowledge that here, with El and her family, I am no longer alone. The darkness cannot reach me now. It's hours later when the logs from the fire finally burn out, though their warmth stays with me for a long, long time.

23
Waggo Woggo

A few weeks later and the dog Lulu from El's cousin's house has inspired me. I'm addicted to them now—dogs—addicted to searching them up on the Internet, visiting them in shelters, and smiling at every pup, canine, and waggo woggo I see. "I am genuinely obsessed with dogs," I tell my dog-loving friend, Erin. "I don't know what to do about it."

Erin volunteers to help me find one. "It has to be perfect," I tell her, "but a little soulless, too. Does that make sense?" I'm not sure Erin understands, though still she agrees to help.

We send each other dog texts on the daily. "How is this one?" she asks, a picture of a bright chubby corgie attached. "Too small," I say. "Too soulful. I need more dog, less soul." "I get you," Erin replies, looping me a link to a giant lab mix later that day. "Perfect," I say, "except my dog can't have energy. I don't have energy. I need one that will match my energy levels."

While inspired by Lulu, my newfound love of doggos is amplified by Erin, who exudes the love, praise, and brightness of a pup in every interaction she has. "I love Erin," I tell El as we drive together one evening, up and down the streets of rain city. "I want to be just like her when I grow up."

It's a while before I do find a dog—bright, happy,

wonderful, and, yes, a little bit soulless—though the search catalyzes my friendship with Erin, who's young and true and wise beyond her years. Through Erin, I learn to love openly and honestly, joyfully and unconditionally, in the way every single dog naturally loves the people around them.

"I have a question for you," I pose to Erin one night while leaning against the walls of my bedroom. I'm caught deep in thought and need a friend to dig in with. "You up for it?"

"Yeah, what's up?"

"Not much, just thinking," I say, coming more alive with each word. "Do you ever wonder if death is as much a blessing as life is?"

Erin takes a moment to respond. "Sometimes, yeah. I think if someone is really sick, death can be a blessing."

"Sure," I reply, "sure. I've been thinking lots about Josh lately—his journey and struggle and diagnoses—and I wonder if God ever calls people home out of mercy, out of some kind of divine love for His children that supersedes any earthly love we know of." Erin and I pause to let the idea sink in.

"I think," Erin begins, "that's a beautiful way to look at it. For me, I believe God has a special place for the people who struggled with mental illness and then took their own lives. I think those people were chosen to play a special role on this earth, because it's impossible for me to believe God allows mental illness and suicide on purpose."

Quiet reigns, and Erin takes advantage of the silence. "What I'll say is, I agree with you," she continues. "For your brother's case, perhaps death was a blessing. I think that just proves God has a plan for him that's greater than we know right now."

Then, "I fully, strongly believe that when someone takes their life God is there, waiting for them. He is waiting to love and accept them with open arms."

Quiet returns, and in that fullness an image, a vision surfaces. In it I see Josh, I see my brother, and, it seems, one other…

Josh, wily hair and bloodshot eyes, walks home, his pale form abreast on clouds of silver—

Nearing nearing nearing the throne of God—

God turns at Josh's approach and stands, a grand

headdress of red and gold feathers adorning His beautiful head—

God raises a mighty chaffed staff and approaches Josh, truth and justice raging hot in His eyes—

But then God stops, relaxes, leaves His staff floating, directed skywards, and steps down to meet His son, tears filling those soft, perfect eyes, blue and blue as all the oceans—

Our God of Light wraps, embraces Josh, and my brother is shrouded in robes of white, a covering of water, soft and blue, that holds and hems, wraps and restores, quietly erases each tattooed tear on my brother's tired, pale face—

Tears flow unashamedly, though most belong to God, to His angels, to Josh's loved ones who stand here and there and encircle him round about, and—

The scene continues and fades, leaves a song of peace, comfort, blue and gold on my weary heart:

Josh, I weep. *My brother.*

Though for years I've searched, I've found and know it now:

You are home. Home and home and home at last.

Epilogue
Hope

24
Raw Wings

My Savior's love is always with me. Through grief, travail, and great darkness He's carried me, cocooned me in His arms and held me, raw and sticky, until I grew strong enough to stand on my own.

I fly now, clothed in His grace. His wings speak a lightness on my back; within those airy feathers I find healing, I find peace. I find a godly hope and strength to carry on.

I pray to my God often, begin to thank Him for the light and love He has poured into my life. Often, those words turn to tears, cries to sobs, as I consider what He has done for me. In love and mercy He sent His Son, the Savior of the world, to cry and fall and bleed on earth. The Son of Righteousness, the very One who rose from the grave the third day with healing in His wings—rose, rose, never to fall again.

I find now, day by day, that in His arms I am found; in His arms I am light.

I am made infinite and whole once again.

This day is for my Savior, in whom I am all that I am—

In whom I extract the promise of all that I can be.

Thank you, Lord.

Thank you.

25

In Waves

Held in love and prayer by friends who are gods, saviors to me, I pen a poem to try to capture the hope they've restored to me. My efforts are paltry; brash; imperfect—but fitting.

I title it "In Waves" and address it to my friends:

In Waves

Friend,
You called my name upon the waters
Within the storms and glooming night
'Midst torrid waves I saw your image
A gleaming, stalwart, glorious light

You called and while I heard no words
Nor dictum to annul the waves
I found in you my hope, my beacon
Through you, my friend, my Savior came

He bore no gifts of size nor weight
But walked, hands empty, at His sides
While at His back crashed waves of thunder
His quiet voice quelled anxious tides

"My child, do not be afraid
For God the Lord is with you now
He brings you strength and offers comfort
And within me, His grace abounds

"I know at times it's dark, unclear
But promise it will be okay
Though now, for hours, you've walked in darkness
You'll tread with me in light today"

Then scarred palms open, eyes alive
My Savior neared my wayward ship
He stood and beckoned me to follow
To walk and place my trust in Him

I stepped then stopped and looked, afraid
To wonder why, of me, he'd ask
To step in water, storm a-raging
While all the world glowed wild black

But fixed my gaze on Him, I did
Away from all that raging sea
And in His eyes I saw a vision:
A lighted confidence in me

His words they echoed through my mind
"My child, do not be afraid"
In trust I stepped out on the water
And as I did, those wild seas tamed

"Do not give fear to storming tides"
My Savior started, with a smile
"For while they'll harry for a season
You'll find it's only a small while

"Then, once your splendid journey's through
You'll gain reward beyond your dreams
Not treasures of the earth, nor silver
But God's gift saved for kings and queens"

He spoke on but His words faded
Obscured within a dreamy mist
I woke within my living bedroom
With one desire, one tiny wish

"Be thou with me through all my life
My Lord, I ask of thee," I prayed
"For all I have—my hope, my reason
Is here today, before thee laid"

I rose in earnest, not alone
For friends and saviors stood with me
Through them God's led me, helped me, loved me
In the same way that he's leading you

I pray you'll find Him, know Him, see
That His love is always near
You're not alone—we're here, we're with you
Our one brave hope trumps every fear

There's hope beyond the darkness, friend. Take it and walk; take it and breathe.

Please know you're worth this life and so much more.

Amber

Fin

"The reality of the Resurrection of [our] Savior overwhelms our heartbreak with hope because with it comes the assurance that all the other promises ... are just as real—promises that are no less miraculous than the Resurrection. We know that [Christ] has the power to cleanse us from all our sins. We know that He has taken upon Himself all our infirmities, pains, and the injustices we have suffered. We know that He has 'rise[n] from the dead, with healing in his wings.' **We know that He can make us whole no matter what is broken in us.** We know that He 'shall wipe away all tears from [our] eyes; and there shall be no more death, neither sorrow, nor crying, neither shall there be any more pain.' We know that we can be 'made perfect through Jesus ... , who wrought out this perfect atonement,' if we will just have faith and follow Him.

"I testify of the reality of [Christ's] Resurrection. Jesus Christ lives, and because of Him, we will all live again. In the name of Jesus Christ, amen."

Paul B. Johnson, "And There Shall Be No More Death"
Words spoken Sunday, April 3, 2016

Copyright 2020 © Amber Everett Books

www.ingramcontent.com/pod-product-compliance
Lightning Source LLC
Chambersburg PA
CBHW071929020426
42331CB00010B/2779